Valerie Shereck is a retired certified nurse practitioner, educator, and clinical nursing instructor. She is a certified yoga instructor and continues to teach yoga in her studio, which she shares with her artist husband. She is a devoted and award-winning gardener, avid reader, birdwatcher, animal lover, and crossword enthusiast.

This collection of poetry is dedicated to all beings: two-legged friends and four-legged friends. Those with wings and mostly, to the flowers.

Valerie Shereck

# CONVERSATIONS WITH FLOWERS

AUSTIN MACAULEY PUBLISHERS™

LONDON • CAMBRIDGE • NEW YORK • SHARJAH

**Ordering Information**
Quantity sales: Special discounts are available on quantity purchases by corporations, associations, and others. For details, contact the publisher at the address below.

**Publisher's Cataloging-in-Publication data**
Shereck, Valerie
Conversations with Flowers

ISBN 9798889108467 (Paperback)
ISBN 9798889108474 (ePub e-book)

Library of Congress Control Number: 2023916607

www.austinmacauley.com/us

First Published 2024
Austin Macauley Publishers LLC
40 Wall Street, 33rd Floor, Suite 3302
New York, NY 10005
USA

mail-usa@austinmacauley.com
+1 (646) 5125767

In gratitude to all those who helped support me in this publication. Special thanks to Marc Shereck, Jennifer Chappell, Angie Adams, Liz Stedem, Jeffery Payne, and Jennifer Mulson.

# Table of Contents

| | |
|---|---|
| The Poet's Daughter | 11 |
| Joy | 12 |
| Conversations with Flowers | 14 |
| The Path | 16 |
| Split Ends | 17 |
| How I Am | 18 |
| Sacred Space | 19 |
| Words like an Arrow | 20 |
| Monday Mail | 21 |
| Milagro | 23 |
| Unanswered Song | 25 |
| Together | 26 |
| Vulnerable | 27 |
| Anonymous Protector | 29 |
| My Friend | 31 |
| Peace in this New World | 32 |

Hope                                34

The Call of Yoga                    35

In the Comfort of My Dogs           36

Bookmarks                           37

May Day                             39

Moments                             41

Monument Valley Park                43

Poverty                             45

Things That I Have Planted          47

Scar Tissue                         49

A Life                              50

Gentle Rain                         51

Tea Leaves                          52

White Orchid                        53

Incidental Garden                   54

Seeds                               56

Standing Still                      57

To Be Again                         59

Benevolence                         60

Garden of My Soul                   61

# The Poet's Daughter

Born too soon
Leaving the safety of the womb
Small and petite
But not fragile

Emerging into a world
Of words and wonder
Initially, unable to speak
Due to a small birth defect
Yet soon
My voice was released

You encouraged me
To read and write
Embracing the stories
The telling
Sometimes shocked and embarrassed
By my candor

Yet you knew
I was the Poet's daughter

# Joy

My four-legged friend
Who I missed seeing for days
The snow, cold, and ice
Kept you from laying on the grass
A favorite pastime of yours
Your golden coat warming in the sun
Each day as I walked past
You always came to greet me
Awakening even from your slumber
Your stiff limbs slowly arising
As you ambled toward me
I would caress and stroke you
With my hand and my voice
Conveying my love and warmth
Today as I walked by
You were outside with your master
He was shoveling snow
You were unfettered and free
I waved to you both
Somehow you knew it was me
My presence, my essence
Despite your aging eyes
You bounded across the street

Full of unabashed joy
Jumped into my arms and greeted me
Smiling, you then
Laid down and rolled in the snow.

# Conversations with Flowers

In silent communion
I greet you
Usually in the early morning hours
When you have rested

The morning dew covers you
You are at peace
Resting in your splendor

I tend to you
Dead-heading, weeding
Cultivating the soil
That surrounds you
The bed where you lay

I speak to you tenderly
Not with words but
With my touch

You speak to me
With your dry or damaged leaves
Asking me to remove them

Asking me to release
The beauty within

I cannot protect you
From the elements
The torrential rain, the hail
The devastating heat
But I can be there
Talking to you
In silent communion and
Conversations with my flowers

# The Path

Rock strewn path
Asking for silence and prayer
In this beautiful space
Surrounded by mountain peaks
And golden aspen

The call
To serenity and peace
As I walk the path
The Labyrinth inward

To the center of my core
Which I have neglected lately
Seeking solace elsewhere

But now in this time and space
Close to nature
Clarity arises
Walking slowly and meditatively
To the center and back
In silence and in prayer

# Split Ends

Trimming my hair
The ragged edges
So that they
Can grow
And flourish

Just as I want
To trim
The ragged edges of us
And our disconnect

Needing to mend
And grow
The rift between us

Needing to heal
The gap
Of our space apart
Our disconnect
Split ends

# How I Am

You ask me
Lovingly
How I am

I pause
And think to myself
Thanking you
For noticing
For asking

How I am
And
I say to you
I do not know

# Sacred Space

How can I not be at peace?
In this sacred space
The light, ever-changing
The clouds
That drift by

Sounds are muffled and mute
Except for the tinkling
Of the bells
As they answer to the wind

I see the wildlife
All around
Foraging for food
I am at peace
In this sacred space

# Words like an Arrow

Like an arrow
Through my heart
Your words wound me
But they do not kill me
Or my spirit

Unconditional
Is my love for you
Your words have
Wounded me
I need to heal

Your words
Challenge me
Make me wonder
what I have done
to create
the hurt that you feel?

Like an arrow
Through my heart
Your words wound me
But create an opportunity
Of healing

# Monday Mail

Every Monday
We could expect it
In our inbox
"Monday mail"
You called it

Today I found your
Last Monday mail
Which you wrote
The day before you died

Reading it
Even after fourteen years
I cried

How I miss
Monday mail
Your ebullient spirit
Your ability to spar
With us all

Your knowledge
Your wisdom

All that you had
To offer

I miss you
So much
And Monday mail.

# Milagro

Tin bird in a tree
A milagro
The sweet remembrance of times past
Times spent in sacred spaces

Alone yet waiting for
Others to come
Silver bird
You have a new place
A new environment

Alone except for the clear
Glass globes with feathers
That surround you
Perhaps your friends
You are waiting
For them to come

Your destiny and legacy
In this world
Atop the tree
Chosen somehow

To protect, guide and heal
To help achieve peace
Tin bird in a tree

# Unanswered Song

Trying to reach out
But not being heard
Feeling as if
I am singing
An unanswered song

Writing the words
Singing the words
They are not listening

To this unanswered song

# Together

Seeing the turtle doves last night
It is said they mate for life
Watching them
Touching so artfully
They flitted and flirted
So tender was their touch
Reminding me of you
Of your tender touch
Your signature smell
Your gentleness,
Your kind soul
Without you by my side
I realize that I
Am just half of what
We are together
An hour away from you
Seems like an eternity
Yet sometimes
We need our space
Away but together
Always

# Vulnerable

.

Open to prey
We go about our lives
Vulnerable

In nature, so true
It has always been
The predator
And the prey

So today
A small squirrel
Lost its life
Subject to prey

A hawk
Large and looming
Set down

The crows
Somehow protective
Shrieked out
Their cries resounded

Despite the clamor
We could not save you
Small squirrel

# Anonymous Protector

Dusk, setting sun
Rising moon
You saw them
Two young deer walking

On a late fall evening
The air was warm
An Indian summer

So they sauntered
These deer
Unafraid and unaware
Of the danger and risks
Of walking on a busy thoroughfare

You, silent stranger
Protector
Gained their confidence
Walked alongside them
With your headlamp

With hope and grace
You walked out into the street

As cars approached
Risking your life
To protect them

These deer trusted you
As they strode out
And crossed the street
Unaware of the danger
At peace
With their protector

# My Friend

Now forty years later
I find that you are gone from me
My friend
Who I somehow thought would
Be with me forever
How naive I was

I didn't tend to our relationship
Neither did you
But I was the tender
So, what to do?

# Peace in this New World

It is Sunday, mid-November
Early morning,
Yet light
The streets are deserted
The trees almost bare
I have to wait at the traffic light

I contemplate the neighborhood
So changed
Yet somehow feeling the history
Of the places
Nostalgia creeps in

My first time in the beautiful
Nave of the church
In almost two years

So changed
Blocked pews
Social distancing
Masks

The beauty of the stained glass
The silence is deafening
No music, no organ
No singing

The all too familiar service somehow lacking
What?
Solace and sanctuary

The offertory gone, and just a wooden box
With slats represents
The way to show gratitude

So much change
So much loss
How can I find some peace
In this new world?

# Hope

As the day dawned
Illuminating the hallowed ground
Where our ancestors
Fought many battles
Not of war, but of words

Your words
Rang out and sang to us
All of us were weary
Of the hate-filled rhetoric
We had heard this before
Which invoked fear in us

Today you brought us hope
With your healing words
As the sun shone
On a bright new day

With your healing words
You sought to soothe our wounds
And beckoned us to join you
In this fight
For a united nation

# The Call of Yoga

Sunlit studio
I light the candle
Turn on the music
And lay down in Shavasana
I let the music, the light
And the skies surround me
As my body awakens to
The call of Yoga
The need to find
My space, my strength and
My balance
As I surrender
To the call of Asana
And pranayama
Each day is new
Each day unique
A meditation in itself
This dance
This vinyasana
The call of Yoga

# In the Comfort of My Dogs

How do I heal?
After a tremendous hurt
Pain so deep
That I feel
I may not recover

Yet here they are
These shiny black and brown creatures
They sense my pain

And reach out to me
In their own way
They nuzzle me
They comfort me

They are beside me
I am here
In the comfort of my dogs

# Bookmarks

There are so many of them
In my life
Some are left there
To mark my place in time

Was I just starting
Or nearly finished
Or was it meant to
Mark a certain quote or poem

These bookmarks
Were often gifts
Some handmade
Perhaps drawn
Pieces of art
Knitted or crocheted

Some are from foreign lands
One a family heirloom
Yet given as a gift

Bookmarks
Placed to create
A space in time
Often reflecting on what is on the pages
They divide and separate
Spaces in our lives
Bookmarks in time

# May Day

Normally a time for baskets of flowers
Delivered to the neighbor's doorstep
A time for spring
Hope and renewal

Today I found you
Tiny dead bird
Lying peacefully
Beneath the covers
Of the bird fountain

There you were
Somehow well preserved
So protected and safe
Perfect in every way
Tiny dead bird

You found a sweet haven
A place to rest
From the turmoil
Not immune
To the apocalyptic times

May Day
Celebration of life and renewal
Or a call for help?
May your sweet tiny soul
Rest in peace
On this May Day

# Moments

Finding peace in this world
Is a treasure
That comes upon us
In rare moments

Perhaps just sitting
In the garden
With a hummingbird so close
You could almost touch it

Or a soft breeze flowing across
Your face
On a hot summer's day

Your elderly dog
Somehow romping
And even bounding with
Her younger sister

Your children finding their
Places in the world
Despite some turmoil

Your spouse of three decades
Immersing himself
In his art
His passion, his calling

Finding peace in this world
Just moments at a time

# Monument Valley Park

Stones and rocks
Line the path
As we walk
Along the dry creek

A place for healing
So many memories
Today as I walked
The whole path
With my dear friend.

This path
So dear to me
Memories of being there
With my children
And others

Running there for
Miles and miles
Training for marathons
An escape

Summer and winter
Spring and fall
Snow, rain, and hail
Could not deter me

This path
Healing took place here
I walked, ran
And laid down on the grass
Sweet healing path

# Poverty

Somehow reminded of a time
Of poverty
Unable to create a meal even
With little to nothing in the pantry

There was Pet milk for the baby
Potatoes
Milk perhaps, a soup of sorts

No meat
Our ribs were showing

A mattress on the floor
No bed
The baby
Slept in a drawer

Yet we were happy
We had shelter
And hope for the future

I boiled the diapers and hung them
On the line
And then they froze

We were humbled
Yet resilient
Never again
We made our way

# Things That I Have Planted

Three Aspen
Two blue spruce
A Russian olive
And a yellow rose bush

Things that I have planted
All of you
are thriving

The Russian olive is not near
Yet, I know that Dad's spirit is
Watching over her
As he always did

So diligently
For so many years
I, too continue
To tend you
Watering, pruning, fertilizing

Watching over
These symbols of my love
Things that I have planted
For all of you

# Scar Tissue

Scar tissue
Remnants of the past
Old wounds, old injuries
Long forgotten
But not

There in the recesses
Of our minds
And our bodies

Painful to recall
So repressed
Not wanting to
Revisit the pain

The wound that
Wouldn't heal
It is there
Scar tissue

# A Life

Sisters of charity
Morning prayers
Starched collars and white uniforms
Order and control
Lessons learned

Standing at attention
Yes sir, no sir
Ready for inspection
Rules and rituals
Discipline and duty

Salutes to the sun
Asana and Pranayama
Bending like a willow
Breathing in and breathing out
Learning to flow like a river

All these precepts
Gathered together
Molding me, into
What I have become

# Gentle Rain

Healing, cleansing rain
A slow steady flow
Not a downpour

Just as my tears run softly down my cheeks
The rain and tears
Soothing the loss
The hole that has been created
With your peaceful passing

Can we learn to accept that
You came to your rest
Leaving this earth
And your beloved life behind

Slowly as the gentle rain
Soaks into the earth
It seems as if
You are sighing
A sense of relief and peace
To leave it all behind

# Tea Leaves

Patterns in a cup
The tea leaves
Tell us a story
Of the past and present and
What is to come
My mother, a seer perhaps
A reader of tea leaves
Able to interpret their meanings
Somehow she knew
What it meant
The foretelling
I may have this legacy
That prophecy, that voice
Sometimes it is a gift
Sometimes it is not

# White Orchid

As the darkness surrounds each day
We acknowledge all the sorrow
So much sadness, grief, and loss
But just as the white orchid
Given in remembrance of you
Shed her last blossoms
There is a hope
Of new growth and
New beginnings
The winter solstice
Will come and then go
The days will elongate
And spring
Will soon be upon us

# Incidental Garden

Who was the gardener?
Who created this incidental garden?
Among the rocks and the bricks
They came
These sweet flowers

First the yellow pansy
So small and petite
Its face painted with a smile

Then came the orange poppy
Surprise, surprise
Slowly the others came

The purple petunia arrived
What!? It is an annual
It doesn't just come back

The alyssum was next
With its small delicate white flowers
In the middle
Holding them all together

Finally the snapdragons
Smaller and more petite than usual
Smattered here and there
Vibrant colors; coral and hot pink

Where did these flowers come from?
Nestling there, safe and secure
By the watering cans and the hardy purple salvia
Perhaps it was the birds
Planting their own incidental garden.

Or perhaps it was the wind
Carrying these precious seeds
From other gardens
Who was the gardener?

# Seeds

Gathering seeds
Like the birds
I pluck them
From the flowers, the squash, the milkweed
Ready to be scattered
By my hand or the winds
Just like the birds
I will be waiting
For the seeds to settle
Ready to sleep
In the winter soil
To awaken and grow
In the promise of spring

# Standing Still

In celebration of the summer solstice
I stand still
In Tadasana
Strong and stable

Being
In the moment
Grounded
Feeling my bones, my toes
Digging into
What supports me

I stand still
In awe of the beauty
Of the earth, and all
That surrounds me

Solstice to me
Is also a time of change
From darkness into light
Or vice versa

Yet, standing still
I am grounded amidst the changes
And shifts of light

I am in awe
Of the beauty
That surrounds me

# To Be Again

Somehow like the deflating of a balloon
All that pressure
All that tension was released

Letting go
Able to just
Inhale and exhale

Surprised
Somehow about this
Not knowing
How much angst I felt

Able to at last
Rid myself
Of the yoke
Of fear and anxiety
Just to be

# Benevolence

How did you know?
What I needed
Kindness
A soft touch, a word
Of sympathy, kindness
And benevolence

You cared for me
Loved me
Never had envy or anger
Just benevolence

So rare
Benevolence

# Garden of My Soul

Many hues of color
Yellow, red, fuchsia, white, pink, and salmon
You have reached your glory
In the last days of fall

Resplendent and proud
Of your victory
Over the virus
The disease
That afflicted you

Somehow
You survived
Stronger and
More beautiful than ever

I tend you
As the days grow shorter
The soil is cooler
You continue to persevere
How I will miss you
Garden of my soul

Made in United States
Troutdale, OR
01/02/2024